Under the Demerara Sun

A Memoir of My Childhood in Guyana

Abigail Satnarine

DEDICATION

To my beloved father, Rev. Jewan Satnarine, whose love
and dedication for my siblings and I have never wavered
from the day we came into this earth until the day he
drew his last breath. Dad, your compassion, love,
humility, and guidance will forever remain in my heart. I
miss you so much each day and the pain of losing you
still stings today. May you rest in eternal peace until we
meet again. To my beautiful mother, Pansy Satnarine, I
am truly in awe of your incredible strength. Thank you so
much for loving and being there for me throughout the
years. You are an amazing Mom and I am so blessed to
have you. I love you so very much. To my gorgeous
little sister, Angela thank you so much for always
listening and encouraging me. You are such a true gem

and I am blessed that God has placed you in my life. I
am so happy for the wonderful journey that lay ahead for
you and my wonderful brother-in-law, Ryan. I know that
you will be the most incredible mother and I can't wait to
hold my precious little niece one day. To my handsome
brothers, Don (aka. Joshua), John and Joel (the three
amigos, as Dad would say, lol). You truly are the most
admirable human beings I know. I am so very proud of
all that you have accomplished and of who you are. I am
so lucky to have you as my brothers and want to thank
you for my three new sisters, Jenelle, Alicia and soon to
be bride, Karolina, who I am extremely grateful for as
well. Now, family gatherings and holidays have gotten so
much more exciting. To my little girl Victoria, you are
the light of my life and the very core of my heart. I am
thankful each day for you. I treasure and adore you in
every way and I am so proud of the smart, kind,

respectful, and loving person that you are. I love you

forever and ever and I hope one day as you read this, that

you'll gain an understanding of that special part of your

history in that great land of Guyana, where your Mom

and Dad was born. To my husband Ralph, thank you for

being by my side throughout our 12 years together and

for being such a great Dad to our little girl.

OH, SWEET GUYANA

Oh, Sweet Guyana,

Land of my birth

Your glorious beauty shines

From the Rupununi River to the Demerara Sea

From atop Mount Roraima

To the Mighty Kaieteur Falls

Oh, Bountiful land

Of bauxite, timber and gold

The summer rain bears down upon

your forests deep and pure

the animals run free and wild

and scatter in the trees

In the deep Savannah

And down the coastal shore

The people work in cane and rice fields

and fish by the sea

They bring home a sweet catch

And in jubilation sing of thee

ABIGAIL SATNARINE   UNDER THE DEMERARA SUN

CONTENTS

ABIGAIL SATNARINE   UNDER THE DEMERARA SUN

ABIGAIL SATNARINE   UNDER THE DEMERARA SUN

PROLOGUE

I was born in the continent of South America, in a little country called Guyana, bordered by the neighboring nations of Venezuela, Suriname and Brazil. Guyana is an indigenous Amerindian term derived from both the Arawak and Carib tribes meaning the "Land of many waters." It is a tropical country, with fertile grounds rich in minerals such as bauxite, gold and aluminum. Guyana's four main rivers, Berbice, Demerara, Essequibo and Corenthye flow mightily throughout its land and into the Atlantic Ocean. It has towering trees and is laden with exotic flowers, fruits, majestic birds and fascinating wildlife. It's an exciting place where the rainforest runs deep and giant species roam free throughout its vast wetlands and Savannah plains.

Home to the largest single drop waterfall in the world, Kaieteur Falls is its shimmering pearl, bringing in tourists from all corners of the globe. But the heartbeat and soul of Guyana is its people, diverse and beautiful from the native Amerindians to the Indo-Guyanese, Afro-Guyanese, Chinese, Portuguese and British Guyanese residents.

Guyana is also the only English speaking country in the South American Continent with some of the dialect in the form of broken English known as Creole. Sadly, many of the native tongues from other lands were lost, wrought through the separation of peoples from their families and homelands and by the forced exportation of slaves on ships and vessels across the seas from Africa to Guyana during the mid 17th Century. Many had to adapt to a new language thrusted on them by the slave owners. Men were assigned to work in the sugar plantation fields while women would serve as cooks or maintain the household duties for the Colonialists.

When the abolition of slavery was passed on May 5th, 1838, Indentured Servitude was introduced and Recruits from various parts of India, China, and the Caribbean worked along with the British Empire to gather laborers to Guyana. *The toils, sweat, and tears against the harshness of the sun by grandparents and parents in Guyana's tropical climate will never be forgotten. For it was through their beaten scars, aching backs, blistered hands and feet, their hard work and sacrifice that shaped this nation to what it is today. A country, still evolving, still growing, still learning, never to repeat the dark transgressions of its past again.*

Yet, some remnants of their cultural history were preserved and transferred from one generation to the next. It was this uniqueness culminating into 'One People, One Nation, One Destiny' that surmises Guyana today. It's a multi-ethnic community that's alive with art and song and dance, all woven together with stories upon stories of strength, honor, perseverance and pride... pride in the land that

they   call   their   home.   Here   is   *mine*...

"Small days is still on meh mind. Small days is a good good time."

■ Guyanese Folk Song

1 THE BOOKSHELF

There once lived a young mother and father in the upper floor of a tiny wooden house with their newborn baby girl…and her paternal grandparents. The house was surrounded by a light gray wooden fence with a small iron gate in front. Two hibiscus plants towered on either side of its entrance bearing beautiful flowers of red and gold. There was a cashew tree to the left. Adjacent to the tree was an open pipe with an area for washing clothes or watering the plants. A long tube ran from the pipe through a slit in an enclosed shower stall so the adults could bathe in private. The children however, would fill buckets of water and wash themselves with a big soapy sponge outside in the yard. Next to the shower grew a towering five-finger (star fruit) tree that turned a deep gold or orange when ripe.

Our house was built on stilts to keep out the rising flood waters during the rainy season. It was raised above ground by a few round cement posts that held up its frame and accessed by two wobbly, squeaky wooden stairs on either side. A small hammock was tied to two of the posts underneath the house and opposite of the mango tree in the front yard creating a perfect little shade from the heat and a sweet little spot to rest or read. Inside of the house, a small corridor was used as a living space. It connected two bedrooms, one for her parents and the other for her grandparents and led to the kitchen.

In one of the rooms, nestled comfortably on her parents' bed, beneath peach colored sheets, lay a tiny little girl who was fast asleep. She was a vision of innocence and beauty and a delight to all who drew near. She cooed, smiled and played with every kindred spirit that visited her and was deeply loved by her family.

One day, a dangerous and powerful storm came by. It brought with it a rolling thunder that rippled across the sky, bolts of lightning that flashed frantically, a torrential downpour which sounded like heavy pellets on their zinc framed roof and a strong fierce wind. It violently shook the small wooden frame of the house. Suddenly, a loud bang was heard along with the sound of falling objects. It was coming from the direction of the bedroom where the child was.

Then it came. The wailing cry of a baby echoing throughout the house. In the kitchen, it was met with the terrifying shriek of the mother, screaming, "No!" as she ran to where the baby lay. The father leapt from where he was and reached the bedroom at the same time. What they saw next, left them in complete shock. They covered their mouths in awe and were astonished at the sight.

There she was, their little girl, their pride and joy, in the center of the bed. The bookshelf had shaken during the storm and was leaning forward. All the books, even the heavy, voluminous ones had fallen on the bed. But to their amazement, they were scattered all around the baby without touching her. Her little self was unscathed and unharmed. Her mom picked her up with tears in her eyes and her Dad said a silent prayer of thanks. This was indeed a miracle. That baby was *me*.

\

2 BLACKOUT

I could feel the sway of the mango tree as its branches bent towards me, bringing with it a sudden coolness in the air. The day quickly turned into night as the gloomy clouds rolled in. Mama called out to me and in no time, I was running up the wooden stairs of our little house and through the door to where she sat tending to one of my younger siblings. The thunder roared as a flash of lightning burst across the sky. It continued for a half an hour while I ate and prepared for bed. I pulled up the covers tight and peeked from the corner of my eye as the light from the little lamp flickered on and off. Another boisterous roar came, this one louder than the rest. The heavens opened and several bolts of blinding white lights lit up the night. Suddenly, heavy raindrops began pounding the pavement outside. Within a few seconds, all went dark.

I was frightened. "We having a blackout, go quick and light a match!" my mom shouted to my father in her natural Guyanese dialect. Dad found his way into the kitchen, reached into a drawer and pulled out the little white and red matchbox. He quickly struck the black strip across its side and the matchstick flared to life. He then grabbed the dark gray kerosene lamp that hung just above the stove and lit it. Next, he grabbed a few candles to brighten up the place a little more.

The strong odor of the kerosene and the sweet scent of the candles intertwined and wafted through the air as Daddy carried them through the house. Holding the lamp in one hand, he carefully placed a candle in the far corner of the room. Then he sat on the edge of my bed, gently patted my head and wished me goodnight.

Instantly, I felt better. I was no longer scared. The room felt warm and comfortable. The raindrops eventually slowed into a soft pitter patter. Sleep came quickly as I closed my eyes and drifted off into dreamland.

3 NANI

My Grandmother's hands were smooth and shiny as she lit the wicks of the oil-filled *diyas* and carefully placed them in my tiny palm. Just a few hours ago, we were having fun shaping them into perfect little bowls until we set them down in the sun to dry. As the evening fell, we began placing the little earthen jars around our little house. We followed a parallel route from our wooden staircase and towards the path where our cashew and guava trees stood on opposite sides. I heard the rustle of their leaves amidst the cool evening breeze, their overarching branches almost reaching out to greet me with a nod as I continued placing my little lamps here and there.

When, we reached the front of our gate where my favorite flowers grew, the scent of red hibiscus blooms filled the air and I stopped for a moment, inhaling its fragrance. We placed even more *diyas* around our yard, and then stepped back in awe. It was an amazing sight. There stood our modest home, illuminated by little lamps, underneath a canopy of stars and beneath the silvery glow of the moon. There was nothing more spectacular in the eyes of a child for today was Diwali, the festival of lights and an occasion for celebration with all sorts of sweets. It was a delightful and joyous experience for me who, as a little girl, eagerly awaited and celebrated this important occasion with my grandmother. For although my mother and father was bringing me up in the Christian faith, I understood the religious significance it held for my grandmother and I was grateful at such a tender age to witness her faith and devotion and even more so for the deep bond that it created between us.

Fond memories of my uncles also resurface each time the festival *Phagwa* comes around. On one occasion when I was about six, I was playing in the yard behind our house and peeked through the rifts of our wooden fence to see my *chachas* (uncles) carrying buckets of water and colored powder. They were hardly recognizable with their red and green hair and orange and yellow faces. Their clothes were a mix of purple and gold. It was truly an incredible sight. I wasn't scared but hid as they entered the gate for I knew what they were up to. My swift little feet ran when they found me and I squealed with glee as they doused me with water and all sorts of colorful dyes. I would pretend to be mad but inside I was smiling. I was having the best time a kid could have. They would then give me the most wonderful hugs along with a Phagwa

greeting before they parted and continued their way,

jovially calling out my grandmother's name to perform

the same ceremonious act.

4 MASHRAMANI

'Mash' is one of the biggest and most jubilant celebrations in Guyana marking the day in which Guyana became a Republic in 1970. You can feel the momentum and excitement building up way before February 23rd rolls around because that's all the neighborhoods will talk about from 'morning til night'. Uncles were busy building carts or makeshift tents, some cooked but mostly it was the Aunties who were delegating responsibilities regarding the food preparations. Some of the ladies proudly displayed their artistic and sewing skills. Heaps of cloth were brought in to make colorful costumes of all different designs. Some men were already beginning to *'sport'* drinking their rum and playing checkers or chess. As the day approaches, *tassa* drums grew louder slowly rising to match the excitement of the people.

Mashramani, as originated in the Amerindian-Arawak native tongue means, "a job well done." When Mash finally arrived, my heart pulsated with excitement. My family got dressed in our Sunday best and eagerly left the house. Going up the road, we passed people with carts and baskets selling all sorts of enticing foods and pastries. There were those staple Guyanese foods like Chowmein and Fried Rice along with Chicken, Goat, Duck, Beef, Fish or Shrimp Curries with a side of Dahl and Rice. Other savory treats include Chesse Rolls, Phoulourie, Egg Ball, Potato Ball and Cassava Ball with its mango sour, tamarind or pepper sauce. Then not too far ahead, our mouths would water even more for the sweet delicious Pine Tarts, Salara, Chinese Bean cake, Cassava Pone, Methai, Sugar Cake, or Fudge. I loved the warm flavors of the hot milky Sweet Rice mixed with cinnamon and the Vermicelli cake with raisins. I also noticed other kids happily indulging in their favorites like Custard, Ice Block, Fluty, Ice Cream of all different flavors and my favorite, the snow cone mixed with carnation milk and drizzled with a delicious cherry flavored syrup.

When the people felt a bit thirsty, we would see guys with large machetes called '*cutlasses*' skillfully chopping the tops of coconuts so that they could enjoy a refreshing drink right out of the fruit along with the sweet jelly inside. Freshly pressed cane juice was just ahead and turning right would be that delicious homemade Mauby and freshly brewed Sorrel drink.

Blankets were spread on pavements with patriotic and novelty items for sale. Some had tents or even donkey carts selling clothing, flags, hats and blankets with the colors of the Guyanese flag or the Coat of Arms carefully stitched on.

Guyana's rich diversity and heritage was evident as well. In the market were Amerindian and Portuguese cloths and trinkets, Chinese porcelains, African beads and *dashikis* and Indian bracelets, as well *saris* and *shalwars* as well. Those were just some of the goods being displayed during today's Mash celebration.

Music would blare through speakers coming from the neighbor's yard to down the street to the stage where singers and musicians were busy playing a mixture of African and Indian songs on *tassa* and steel drums. Calypso, Soca, Dancehall, Reggae, Chutney Bacchanal, Bhangra, and Hindi songs were played as people danced past sunset and into the wee hours of the morning.

There would also be singing, dancing, art, and poetry competitions. At the end of the night, there would be a plethora of awards including those for the best float, costume design and band. There would also be a new king and queen of Mash.

The parade had just started and the crowd formed a line on both sides of the main road. Soon, proud Guyanese men and women in shiny, glittery elaborate costumes with painted faces of red, green, black, white and gold all symbolizing the unity of the people of Guyana came prancing down the middle of the roadway. What I loved seeing most was the feathers that were etched on their headpieces, on the side of their masks and flamboyantly displayed on their clothing or on either side of their outstretched arms. It was like watching a gleaming bird, invincible and ready to soar. I was mesmerized and completely in awe of the beauty that surrounded me.

Yet the best part of the night was going to the fair that usually came to town on Mashramani. I found the greatest thrill in attending the rides and participating in all the games and activities. The Merry Go Round and the Ferris Wheel were my favorites. I pleaded and begged my grandmother to go on it. She urged me to be patient. "Yuh jus eat gyal, wait til yuh food settle in yuh stomach nah," she said. But I was too anxious and hesitant and didn't want to miss out on all the fun. Later that night, as I crept into my grandmother's bed, exhausted and tired from a long day of festivities, I felt my stomach churn. My grandmother was right after all. But the sights, smells, sounds, and excitement of that day had already taken root, no matter where the future takes me, its joyous memories were etched in my conscience forever.

OL'HIGUE
By Wordsworth McAndrew

Ol' woman wid de wrinkled skin,
Leh de ol'higue wuk begin,
Put on you fiery disguise,
Ol'woman wid de weary eyes
Shed you swizzly skin.

Ball o'fire, raise up high
Raise up till you touch de sky,
Land 'pon top somebody roof
Tr'ipse in through de keyhole-poof!
Open you ol'higue eye.

Excerpt from the Poem Ol'Higue by Wordsworth
McAndrew[1]

---

[1] Wordsworth, McAndrew. "Ol Higue" Cultural Folklore by Petamber Persaud, *Guyana Times International*, February 28th, 2014: Accessed: September 16, 2019. https://www.guyanatimesinternational.com/cultural-folklore/

5 STORIES

When I was a little girl, I loved to hear stories. I remember sitting by my grandmother's side as she braided my hair and told me stories of long ago. She couldn't read or write but no one could tell a better story. It was fascinating and detailed with a good plot, had unexpected twists and turns and would keep you on the edge of your seat. When she was finished, you'd feel it's effect for days.

Sometimes, I'd sleep in my grandmother's room. She had a little ritual where she'd oil her legs from her knees down, stretch, light the *argarbatti,* a type of sweet smelling incense, then go to bed. I'd watch her keenly then curl up next to her to listen to her stories. Some were pretty scary like that of the Old Higue, a witch like old woman who could turn into fire or fly into your house at night and suck your blood.

In the morning, you'd see the deep dark purplish marks on your arms, neck and legs or feel the burning sensation of the fire and know she had visited that night.

In the evening time, she'd tell me Jumbee stories. Jumbees were evil spirits of the dead who haunted you. Sometimes they'd trick you and laugh or sometimes they'd cause you harm. They lived in dark secluded places, down lonely streets, in burial grounds, and in the top floor of your house. Sometimes they would come down and bother you during blackouts and thunderstorms.

Once, during a powerful storm, I peeked through our window curtains. A bright white light flashed from the sky and there staring back at me was the grim reaper in his dark heavy cloak, watching me with beady eyes and a pitchfork in his hand. He had come for me.

Frightened, I quickly closed the blinds and ran to my bed

hiding under the covers. The next day, I somehow gained

the courage to look out the window again but this time,

he was gone. Was it a dream?

To this day, I am petrified of lightning. But then

again, I'd write or tell the best stories during

thunderstorms. During one particular storm, I placed a

white sheet over my head and body, dabbed white

powder over my face and walked into the room where

my younger siblings were. "Boo, I'd say," causing them

to almost pee their pants. Then when the joke was over,

I'd sit next to them and begin a story...

"It was a dark and frightful night. The howling

winds encircled me and leaves scattered to and fro as I

walked along the lonely road. Suddenly, darkness filled

the sky and the clouds burst open as rain came pouring

down. I continued my path, hoping to find some shelter when I came across an old woman sitting under a Banyan tree. She was wearing a large black hat and when she looked up at me, she gave me a devilish smile. She had just a few teeth, yellowing and crooked. "Are you lost, Dearie? She asked. "Just follow me. I know the place you're searching for." Hesitatingly, I obeyed her. She led me towards an open field and as I got closer, I realized there were grave stones all around. I began to tremble and when I looked up, the woman had disappeared. Instead what appeared before me was a big black cat with large green eyes emerging out of a freshly dug hole in the ground. Looking up at me, it gave a long purr but then baring its teeth, hissed at me like a snake. Horrified, I turned around and ran as fast as my legs could muster. Not looking back even once."

This story alone would cause their faces to light up with excitement and send goosebumps down their spine. Yet each time they heard it, they asked for even spookier details than the last.

My grandmother also relayed Obeah stories. They were even worse than jumbee stories because they involved black magic and people could put a curse on your life. Bad things could happen to you and your family or you could get sick or poisoned and die. Anyone could go to the 'Obeah man' and ask a favor or pay them for an anecdote to carry out their spell.

My father's stories were light-hearted, funny and sometimes teachable. When he returned home from giving his lessons at Secondary School or from preaching at church, my siblings and I would sit on his lap or by his side as he told us Anansi and Brer Rabbit stories. These were cultural treasures, folklores and myths orated through the ages and told from one generation to the next.

His stories also had fictional characters and places. My dad would keep me laughing through the antics of "Sensi Bill and Stupidy Bill." He told stories of animals that taught a special lesson such as the "Fox and the Grapes" in Aesop's fables. But mostly, they were Biblical tales.

Growing up as a minister's daughter, by the time I was five, I knew almost every story in every book of the Holy Bible from Genesis to Revelation. As a Christian, the teachings of Jesus were always the focal point. I especially enjoyed hearing about the parables he told. They spoke of the most important gifts a person could ever own, what could be felt with the heart and not seen.

They were of love and goodness and friendship and being kind in this world.

Although my grandmother and my dad told completely different types of stories, I thoroughly enjoyed them all. Maybe they didn't realize it then but through their stories, they taught me a very valuable lesson, that life will not always be 'a bed of roses', that there will be bad times, scary even, as well as good. Not everyone will be there for you or look out for your best interest. But there are those who will, usually the most important people in your life, who will love you and guide you along as you navigate this life and whose memory… and stories will live on long after the days when they are gone.

6 GUYANA SHOCKS THE WORLD

When I was 14 months old, Guyana was rocked by one of its greatest tragedies known as the Jonestown Massacre. On November 18, 1978 in a remote area of Jonestown, Guyana, a charismatic preacher by the name of Jim Jones who headed the People's Temple Church, carried out a mass suicide by tricking or forcing people to drink cups of Kool-aid mixed with cyanide poison resulting in the deaths of 918 people. The Washington Times documents one person's horrifying account of how Jones prepared his congregation in a sort of ceremony before committing this frightful act:

> Jones held a number of mass suicide rehearsals to see how the crowd would respond, and who would cause him trouble. "And then he made those people line up first," she says. "He figured out that if they killed the children first, then the parents wouldn't have any reason to live. So, he starts with the babies and the people want to believe that this is just another

> rehearsal. For a lot of them it was just surreal. They
> couldn't believe this man, who professed to have their
> best interests in mind, would actually kill them. It
> wasn't until they saw the babies frothing at the mouth
> and writhing that they realized what was going on.
> (Krause, 1978)[2]

The news shook the nation, sent shock waves throughout the world and infamously placed Guyana on the map for decades to come. Years later, survivors of the tragedy or relatives who have lost loved ones are still reeling from the pain of that day. There's no amount of consolation that will take their grief away nor can time erase the memory of those they lost but since then, many have documented their stories and eyewitness accounts. For some, it's an attempt to heal and move forward. For others, it's to caution people of dangerous cults and practices and of leaders claiming to be God as Jim Jones did before he committed a sickening atrocity.

---

[2] Krause, Charles A. "Survivor: They Started with the Babies.", *The Washington Post Foreign Service,* Georgetown, Guyana. November 21st, 1978. Accessed: August 19, 2019.

To this day, many people will utter, "Don't drink the Kool-Aid!" A clear reference to the Jonestown Massacre and a warning to watch out for the sly foxes, the sort of people that would trick and deceive them and offer them false promises.

Today, Guyana is more than just a country stained with the image of Jim Jones. It is a beautiful and fascinating land in the Amazon Basin and a nation moving forward ever closer to a sustainable future, with oil rich reserves and technology that will enable its people to thrive for years to come.

7 GUYANESE WOMEN

As a young girl, I looked up to the women in Guyana with a deep admiration and respect. I was amazed at their remarkable talents and abilities. All around me were strong, successful, intelligent women who surrounded me with love and were a huge part of my life. My mom remains to this day my biggest inspiration and the love I have for her knows no bounds. She raised five children and became an incredible boss in the workforce, all while looking stylish and chic. They say children inherit their intelligence from their mothers. If that is indeed true, then I'm truly honored to be in her shadow.

My Maternal grandmother raised even more children on her own. She loved to sing and her beautiful voice would always soothe and comfort me. As I got older, she would open her yellow book and tell me all about Jesus. She, like my paternal grandmother, never learned to read but knew the Bible well. "You must listen to Jehovah God, she'd say." That was the same woman who worked from day until night to ensure that her children were clothed and fed in order to provide them a happy life.

I'll never forget the day I visited her as a child, she was beating clothes against the rocks by the river, wringing them in her hands so that she could hang them on the line to dry. Then she'd come home and cook the best dinner ever. Her strength and character will always be appreciated and loved. She was not afar off from many of the other women I knew. All around me were women of various backgrounds who were influential leaders and prolific in their field. They were doctors, lawyers and teachers but were also creators, painters, storytellers, dressmakers, embroiders, basket-weavers, homemakers, cooks, business owners and merchants selling everything from goods such as eggs, milk and bread to clothing and jewelry.

There was Sister Joan, who was a member of my dad's church but also a nurse. She was there to help my mother as she delivered a baby at my grandmother's house. My curious cousin and I peeked through the door just as she administered a shot to my mother to ease her pain. A bit traumatized, we quickly closed the door. A few hours later, my little brother emerged with his round beautiful little face. Then he cried and I knew that my third sibling was a healthy and strong baby boy with a good pair of lungs. At that moment, I pondered the miracle of a woman growing a baby in her tummy for nine months, of that woman reeling in pain and of that woman brining new life into this world. It would be a memory etched in my conscious forever. One day, I would experience the same and would admire the undeniable strength of a woman even more.

There was Teacher Lizzy, who took the time to teach us at Sunday School even after a full work week at our Primary School. She was stern at times when we didn't pay attention or forgot our homework but at other times, she was kind and loving. Her pupils later understood the importance of both discipline and love.

The Principal or Headmistress, of our Primary School was also woman. She would visit each class and took the time to know each student. Sometimes she'd quiz you at random times about any given subject. If you did well, she'd pat you on the back on a job well done. If not, she would frown and look at the teacher inquisitively as if they weren't doing their job. She would be the main force behind cultural events, school concerts and plays.

Each morning, she'd lead us into our morning routine, as we stood at allegiance to our flag and sang our national anthem before starting the day.

Once during one of these ceremonies, my dad, who was also a teacher from the secondary school, brought his students to visit our school. They were seated outside on the stands, watching their class playing a relay race game. I happened to sit by the window where I could easily catch a glimpse of my dad. When I decided to take a quick look, my principal caught me and reprimanded me. She had stopped everything and delayed the morning ceremony because I was not paying attention. She told me to stand in front of the class and stick out my right hand. I did as I was told and received two quick lashes on my palm with a stick. I was embarrassed and hurt, even more so because I liked her. Later she realized it was my dad that distracted me and apologized. It was then that I understood everyone's not perfect and I was glad that she took the time to sit and speak with me.

There were some women who didn't have children nor were they in a profession involving them but who were just as strong. Women, to me were not defined by motherhood or by being a wife. Rather, their strength lay in who they were, in their personalities, in their struggles, in their weaknesses, in their accomplishments and in their ability to continue forward throughout it all. Strong women were everywhere. They were nurturing and kind but were also resilient and fierce with fire in their eyes, strength in their bones and perseverance in their blood. Each day, they were busy building and shaping lives while setting examples and trends for other little Guyanese girls…and boys to follow.

8 THE LITTLE GIRL

"Ah watch wah yuh guh na bai! Like yuh head nah good or wah?" Yelled a bicyclist as a man in a vehicle narrowly grazed by him.

"Ay! Cyar yuh tail! Yuh think yuh drive donkey cart out hay? You deh zig zag like wan zipper pon de road!" The man in the car belted.

They tore into each other even more as I diverted my attention to the market just ahead. It was close to 11:00 am and the heat was bearing down. A lady in a straw hat walked by me with a basket in her hand. She was busy inspecting the fruits and vegetables on either side of the wide bridge that led to Patentia's main road. Looking up, I spotted a tiny little girl in a powdery blue dress weaving through the crowd. She was in pigtails held up with two white bubblies. She looked to be about

4 and was looking around frantically and crying.

"Mommy! Ah wheh yuh deh nah? Wah yuh lef me hay

fah? Mommy! Wheh yuh deh?

She disappeared for a second. But then, I caught a

glimpse of her dress near the entrance to the road. She

was about to sprint across where the vehicles were. "Oh

no!" I shouted as I ran towards her. But she continued

and darted in front of a car. My heart raced. Then I heard

the car's loud screeching sound. The crowd came to a

complete halt as their focus turned to the road. Luckily

the commotion between the driver and the cyclist had

slowed the traffic down and the car was able to make a

sudden stop. The girl was safe. Tears of joy rolled down

my face.

Then just as I nearly reached her, someone grabbed her by the arm. "Ah who lil pikney dis?" shouted the lady with the straw hat and basket.

Suddenly, a woman came bursting through the crowd. "Da ah me dauta!" She screamed, running towards the child.

"Mommy!" the little girl cried. "You lef de house and lef me. Meh come look fuh yuh fuh bring yuh back. Daddy sey he sorry Mommy. He nah mean fuh hit yuh. Ah me fault." The woman wrapped the girl tightly in her arms and cried, relieved that she was alive and unharmed.

"Lehwe guh visit Nani, ok?" she softly said. The little girl named Sharda nodded her head and smiled, glad to be with her Mom again.

The people looked on and shook their heads at the young mother and child. The two walked off, lost once more amongst the crowd as they began filling the market again. Up ahead came the sound of blaring horns and

loud voices as another argument ensued between two

other men in vehicles.

9 PATENTIA

I grew up in Patentia Housing Scheme, a small village in a very close knit community near the west bank of the Demerara River. Our home was situated on fertile ground and was surrounded by trees. In good seasons, it was filled with all sorts of fragrant, juicy and tropical fruits such as Sour Sop, Guava, Mango, Five-Finger (Starfruit), Guinep, Sapodilla, Cashew, and Banana. We also had beds of vegetables like Eddo Leaf Bhaji, Cabbage and Carrots.

Vines grew on metal frames raised above them and provided a plentiful supply of Squash, Okra, Baigan (Eggplant) and Bora that we would have fun plucking right off the stems. When they were ripe, we would harvest them in big basins and help our mother wash or chop them up for dinner.

My grandmother kept a Chicken Pen filled with little yellow chicks that we would pick up and play with. The Hen gave us enough eggs to last throughout the month. The neighborhood milk lady or milk man would also come around often and sell us a gallon when needed.

On some days, when my Uncle finished cutting cane for the GUYSUCO sugar estate, the producers of the famous Demerara sugar, he would stop by and bring us a bunch of sweet cane that we would chew in our mouths until all the juices were gone.

During the holidays, Dad would go fishing and returned home with a fresh bucket of crab, shrimp or fish that he caught from the river. Once, he let me accompany him. To my delight, we came back with a bountiful supply of Sheriga crabs that Mom cleaned and curried for a delicious dinner that evening.

Mom would also get flour from the neighborhood shop and would use it to make the fluffiest bake or the soft flakiest paratha roti. Other times, she would use the flour to make the most delicious sponge cake that paired perfectly with a scoop of vanilla ice cream.

At the beginning of our block was our Aunt and Uncle's house who lived in a beautiful two story home with a veranda that overlooked the street. We were not related but were as close as ever. My brother even called them Mama and Papa as we would be there so often. My uncle was a Pastor and a Police Chief in the neighborhood. He was both feared and loved. He sometimes had a serious side while my Aunt displayed a softer personality. Yet, they each loved and treated us as if we were their own.

We loved to visit and spend time with them. Their

home was welcoming and inviting. There was a beautiful dining room area and living room area with lovely paintings that decorated the walls. It was there where my family celebrated birthdays and special occasions. It was where we watched our first television show, The Price is Right. It is where I first saw that handsome gentleman with the swiveling hips, Elvis Presley and got a taste of another musical icon, Madonna on screen.

On some occasions, my Uncle would take us out for a ride in his Jeep. When we got back, my Aunt would already have a delicious meal and dessert waiting for us on the table. Some evenings, my siblings and I would wander about their yard, filling our bellies with the juicy, ripe Jamoon fruit that fell from their tree. We also would play cricket games or spend time with their dogs while the adults settled in front of the television for the beginning of the soap opera, Dallas with their favorite character, J.R. Ewing as the leading man. By the time Falcon Crest ended, it was usually time to head home.

Aunty Jenny (also not a relative) was the neighbor who lived to the right of us. Her house was just like ours except she did not have a fence. In the afternoons, I'd see her sitting on the front steps braiding her daughter's hair into tiny beautiful little braids. Her daughter and I were in the same grade and as we were in the same neighborhood, we quickly became friends as well. Sometimes, I would share the sweetie candies or chico gum that my Nani had brought home from the market. Other times, I would happily sit with them on their stairs and listen as her mom told us jokes and stories. She would even laugh before she finished them. It was the heartiest laugh I had ever heard and it was contagious. Other times, I'd go over by the foot of their stairs and call out to my friend to come down for a nice game of Hopscotch, Jacks, Tag or Holes to play with me and the other neighborhood children. We would run and laugh and play until our energy was spent and the sun began to set. It was only then that our tummies would grumble and we knew it was time to head inside for dinner.

Saturdays were always busy. Mom would be in the yard hanging out clothes, cooking or tending the garden while Dad was preoccupied with fortifying the fence or doing yardwork. Around the neighborhood, youths were riding around the neighborhood on their bicycles, climbing trees to pick fruits or doing yardwork with their uncles and fathers.

Some children were happily enjoying ice-cream cones from the ice-cream truck while others were playing double-dutch outside. My siblings and I were also having fun. We would cast a mini fishnet that the adults had given us into the trench to see how many little silver fishes we could catch. Once we were finished, we would drill two holes in tin cans and attach a string to each end to play a game of telephone.

On Sundays, we would all pile into a neighbor's car or take the bus to Crane church where Dad would lead the congregation into a time of prayer and worship before beginning his sermon. He was a fiery preacher with a resounding voice that spoke powerfully from the pulpit but was the softest and most kindred spirit when he stepped away from the microphone.

When we returned home, we would swing by our Aunt for a Sunday brunch or stay home. A couple of

times after church, he would pick up a big tub of Brown
Betty or Demico Ice Cream to share with us when we
were well behaved in church and then we would come
home, enjoy our treat and relax under the hammock.
Sometimes we would spend the rest of the evening
playing cricket in the backyard with our father or
marveling at the talking parrot that our neighbor brought
by.

On rainy days, we would relax inside as Dad kept
the dial on BBC news or on 1010 Wins to hear the
upcoming weather forecast. 'You give us 22 minutes,
we'll give you the world,' announced the voice of Paul
Anthony every half hour.

When my parents weren't listening to the news,
the radio would be tuned to the Sunday evening theatre
or jazz broadcast. My dad also loved comedy and would
laugh out loud when shows like Abbot and Costello and

Laurel and Hardy would periodically filter through the airwaves.

Easter time in Patentia was also fun. Dad would get to work building us the box or star kites with a vibrant color of our choosing. Mine was usually red and yellow. He would take us in the field and we would hold it with a long string and run to give it some friction. Then watch as it soared into the air with the wind. Sometimes, when the wind picked up speed, it would be so strong that it would pull my little frame up as well. But I held on as much as I could, even bending close to the ground to keep it or myself from flying away.

Once we were finished, we would pick up some of the delicious Chinese food from our village shop and wash it down with a tasty glass of cream soda and carnation milk with crushed ice.

We had one cinema in our district and it is where my dad introduced my siblings and I to Indian movies. I loved catching the latest Bollywood flicks and was enchanted by movie stars such as Sri Devi, Mithun Chakraborty, Amitabh Bachan and Rekha. Their singing, dancing and emotional dramas left me always yearning for more. To this day, I still enjoy sitting back and unwinding to a good Bollywood movie especially on a nice rainy day. It is my ultimate version of Netflix and chill.

Patentia, in my day was a community filled with love. We opened our homes and hearts to those around us. We sang songs and played games. We laughed, loved, and cried together. We shared what little we had, looked after one another and each other's children. It was a place where kids felt safe to run, play and explore their surroundings. We took the time to know each other, to appreciate one another and to grow together. We drew strength from each other and created lasting memories together. It was a joyous time. The good ol' days.

10 SCHOOL DAYS

Each morning at the crack of dawn, the Guinea Fowl would loudly crow, "Cock a doodle doo!" That was our daily que to get ready for school. My brothers and I would then jump into our neatly pressed school uniforms that Mom had laid out for us. I wore a pretty little blue dress with a large white collar. My brother, who was just a year and a half younger, wore a short sleeved white shirt and blue shorts. The youngest was in Nursery school and took the longest to get ready in his white shirt and brown pants. All three of us wore matching white socks and brown sandals which was the typical wear for the rough roads and hot climate.

The schools were so close together that you could walk across the yard between them. But traversing over the narrow bridge to the Primary School was no easy feat. We were terrified of falling into the water and our little feet shuffled slowly across the wobbly wooden boards with no rails on either side. Then, as we reached, we would let out a huge sigh of relief and wait for the crossing guard to get us across the road.

In school, my little brother would color, draw and sing nursery rhymes and songs like, "I am a little teapot." Next door in Form Three, we sat in neat rows doing our Math sums and English essays while the teacher or headmistress walked around.

Corporal punishment was alive and well in school and if we deviated in any way from our lessons or from our code of conduct, our teachers were ready to let us know it with two at least two or three lashes. If children misbehaved at school or were reprimanded for any reason by their teachers, their parents followed suit and wouldn't hesitate to give them a sound discipline with either a belt or stick or whatever they had in hand at home. As such, we adhered to the rigid rules laid out before us. I was a very quiet child who was only punished once but I hated it and wished it never existed for some teachers took advantage of this right on other children.

At lunchtime, we ate whatever our parents packed in our lunchboxes then gathered together outside to jump rope, play Tag or sing "Ring a Ring a Roses." Songs like "Brown Girl in the Ring" and "Rick, Chick Chick," filled the air before the bell rang and school was in session again.

11 BUSH COOK

Devin hauled the big *karahe* from his mother's
kitchen while his little brother Donnel fetched a large
metal spoon to turn the pot. "Put am ova hay right pon de
wood," he instructed his brother.

Donnel, was a sharp-witted boy about my age but
was just as tall his slightly elder brother. He was the
splitting image of his brother with the same dreadlocks
and caramel complexion but complete opposites in
personalities. While Donnel was full of sharp answers
and inquisitive about everything under the sun, Devin
was reserved and observant around others. The brothers

could easily pass for twins and many times I'd see them

playing ball in their yard from my Nani's window. From

a distant, it was unclear who was really who until one of

them would climb their Jamoon tree and whistle in my

direction.

Who bring de match?" Devin called out, already

anxious to get started.

"Ah me get am," my neighbor Mala interjected.

"Ayodese too lil fuh light am!" She proudly declared.

Mala was the eldest and most responsible of the group.

She kept her hair in a long braid in the back while her

little sister Shovna had two cute little braids and a round

chubby face.

Mala scratched the side of the matchbox a few

times until the stick caught a flame then she threw it into

the pile of wood, dry leaves and charcoal on the ground.

The wood began to crackle as the fire roared to life. "Aye

gyal, yuh gah de oil? Mala asked.

"Yeah, e deh right hay!" Her Sister Shovna

replied.

Mala then carefully poured the oil and mixed in

the onions, garlic, herbs and spices that she brought from

her parent's cabinet. "Ok, leh abi put in de chicken now,"

she said handing us a small bowl of marinated chicken

thighs and legs my grandmother had seasoned last night.

She had granted me permission to use it for this little

bush cook with my friends.

The pot made a loud sizzle as Mala carefully

placed the pieces of chicken in the pot. A half an hour

later, I mixed in the rice and black-eyed peas. We poured

in the coconut milk that Devin and his brother brought

along with a nice hot pepper to give it some flavor. Then

we each took turns stirring the pot.

When the water had dissipated and the rice and

chicken were perfectly cooked, Mala grabbed two hand

towels and used them to lift the pot off the flame and set

it aside on the ground. The two boys threw water on the

flame until it went out. Then after the food was warm and

we had washed our hands in the river, we sat together in

a circle as Mala dished out our food in the dry puri

leaves. We gave thanks for the nice meal and ate with our

hands to our hearts content. When we were done, we

rubbed our bellies, clapped our knees like a drum and

sang the chorus to Sundar Popo's Kaise Bani:

> Me and meh darling was flying in a plane
> The plane catch a fire and we fall inside the cane
> Kaise bani
> Kaise bani
> Kaise bani
> Kaise bani
> Phulari bina chatani kaise bani

Phulari bina chatani kaise bani

I beating meh drum and ah singing meh song
I beating meh drum and ah singing meh song
The only thing ah missing is meh bottle ah rum
Kaise bani
Kaise bani
Kaise bani
Kaise bani
Phulari bina chatani kaise bani
Phulari bina chatani kaise bani[3]

---

[3] Lyrics Phulorie Bina Chutney by Sundar Popo (The Legend)
Chutney Classic Lyrics 1980s. Accessed: September 19, 2019

12 THE WEDDING

Today was a big celebration and everyone in the neighborhood was out. There were people everywhere. Some in their front yard. Some on their verandas. Some looking through their windows. Some on rooftops. Even some in trees.

I stood on the top step of Aunty Jenny's house to see above the crowd of people that lined the streets. They held strings of beautiful yellow and red flowers that seem to flow without end. The children threw petals in the air and spun around merrily.

DA DA DA DUM. DA DA DA DUM DUM DUM! went the sound of the Tassa drum as it moved

closer to our block. The drumming was the same familiar
beat that I heard just two nights ago when the bride's
family performed their *Matticore* festivity, a type of
ritual that involved digging up a bit of dirt and giving a
small offering of sweets and spices to the earth for its
blessings on the soon-to-be bride and groom.

In the evening was the haldi ceremony, a hindu
ritual where the young unmarried women, usually the
little sisters, nieces and cousins gathered at the bride's
residence and applied dye or turmeric powder mixed with
water or oil on various parts of the bride's body in
preparation for her wedding day.

Soon the music drew closer and I noticed a throng
of women dressed in long colorful *saris* prancing down
the middle of the street. They were behind the drummers
and were shaking their hips and swaying to the musical
beat. The bridegroom followed them, dressed in his

Sherwani shirt and *Churidas* trouser. He wore a traditional wedding headpiece with the *Sehra* flowers attached to his turban.

The women continued dancing before him to celebrate the occasion as he made his way to his bride's house. Once there, he would sit alongside her and listen to the Pandit as he gave the ceremonial instructions. Together, they would walk around in a circle several times. Then, they would duck under a long sheet and the groom would gently dip his finger in dye and place a red *sindoor*, made up of powdered vermillion in the middle of the bride's forehead to symbolize their marital bond. The Pandit would then pray and the people would sing.

During the evening's festivities, guests would eat the seven curries including the katahar, aloo and pumpkin I saw my aunt dicing up a few days ago. The curries would be served in fresh picked lotus leaves or *puri* leaves as well another one for desserts such as *parsad*, *methai* and sweet rice pudding. There would also be *conkie,* a delicious cornmeal based treat usually wrapped in banana leaves and tied up with strings.

It was then that I realized why my grandmother was preparing all this food and why I had to pick the banana leaves off the tree in our backyard. It was for this great wedding festivity.

I ran down the stairs and weaved quickly through the people until I could see the bride. She was a radiant vision of beauty, more beautiful than any Bollywood actress that I'd ever seen on screen. She wore a red sari, a gold headpiece that hung just over forehead and a simple gold nose ring. She had beautiful collection of gold necklaces that graced her neck along with matching bangles that jingled from her wrists and ankles. Her hands were covered in intricate patterns of *henna* and as I

gazed up at her, she smiled.

As the ceremony commenced, the people

continued partying into the night for there would be more

singing and dancing, what we called 'sporting' for days

or even weeks to come.

13 MY COUSINS

"Ma Riddle Ma Riddle Marie, I come to mend the water wash," was how I greeted my eldest cousin when I reached her house. "Begin!" She said excitedly.

"I have something that is purple outside, and white inside and it is really sweet," she replied.

"A jamoon!" I quickly shouted.

"No," she responded.

"A Starapple?" I asked.

"YES! You got it!" she screamed and threw her arms around me in a tight welcoming embrace.

Her brother was busy with Janey, a thick brown cow that he loved like a pet. He had a large silver pail under her belly and was getting ready to gather some warm milk.

"Aye Bai, A wah ya do deh?" I asked in my native dialect.

"Meh a milk de cow. Yuh wan watch or yuh guh come help meh?"

Reluctantly, I walked over and stooped down to where he was. "Yuh jus hold am like this and pull. But watch out fuh di back foot. He does kick real hard."

"Ok," I said and carefully followed his command.

Swoosh! Swoosh! Went the milk in the pail as it filled to the brim. Its milky froth bubbling on top. My cousin smiled and gave me a pat on the back for a job well done. I felt happy and confident that I could do it all by myself the next time.

"Take this up to Mammy," he said.

I lifted the pail, being careful not to spill the bucket as it swished around in my hand and walked towards the stairs where my Uncle was busy grinding wiri, wiri pepper in a large metal contraption to make pepper sauce. "Hi Uncle," I greeted him. "How yuh do?"

"Meh deh, gyal," he answered. I nodded politely and continued up the stairs to meet my Aunt.

"Hey Abby." Come give yuh Auntie a hug. Yuh a grow so big aready. Like yuh guh reach di top a di lantan pose (light post) soon or wah?"

I felt tall and proud being next to her. She always complimented me and made me smile. She was my favorite Aunty and I was proud to say it. She was busy cooking beef curry, dhal and rice. Her curry was amazing. The meat was so moist and tender and she made my tummy very happy when I ate it. I gave her the milk and she used some of it to make *paynuse*, a delightful dessert made with milk curds. I loved and enjoyed anything my aunt made. Even today, she remains one of the best cooks I know.

Other times when I'd visit my cousins, we'd play games like hide and seek or just relax and tell stories as we ate sweet cherries mixed with sugar from their cherry tree or sliced mango with salt when we wanted a savory snack. It was always fun spending precious time with them. Years later, we would share a special journey together to a distant country called, The United States of America.

14 THE PRESIDENT IS DEAD

One day on August 6th, 1985, the whirring sound of a Jeep drove through our village. It was the same vehicle with the loud megaphone in the back that would roll around on Friday evenings to provide the weekly death announcements. But it was a Tuesday and people were surprised to see it passing through. Soon, we understood why. It was the sudden death of Guyana's President Forbes Burnham who had quickly passed from a heart attack during a throat operation.

"The President is Dead! The President is Dead! it blared through the megaphone.

"The President is Dead!" the people whispered. The news rattled the country to its core. It spread like wildfire and caused an uproar through the town. It was picked up on airwaves and in newspapers around the world including the LA and NY Times. Guyanese both at home and abroad stayed glued to their radios and television sets at the announcement of Prime Minister Hugh Desmond Hoyte as his successor.

By the time December rolled around, everyone, including the kids at school, knew that Guyana was in the middle of a new election. But while the children played together; happily enjoying each other's company regardless of race or creed, the adults were busy using divisive rhetoric, arguing and fighting like cats and dogs over the new impending government. The rising racial tensions and heightened political conflicts that ensued between the two main parties of the People's Progressive Party (PPP) with a majority Indo-Guyanese representation and the People's National Congress (PNC) consisting of a more Afro-Guyanese base, deepened these

divisions as each party was heavily criticized for seeking

to elect a leader that would closely align with and support

their own ethnic segment of the population rather than

the need to invest in policies that would create a healthier

economy and benefit the country as a whole. By the time,

Hoyte was elected, the country was already experiencing

a sharp economic decline from the socialist practices of

the Burnham administration.

Far too often, many of us would go without basic

goods such as flour and rice which were scarce and in

high demand. There would be lines down the block at the

grocery stores and people complained of food shortages

such as wheat flour. A New York Times article noted:

> The goal of his Government, Mr. Burnham said,
> was to create a state of "cooperative Socialism"
> that would remove the vestiges of Guyana's
> former British colonial rule, which ended in 1966,

> free it from alignments with foreign powers and give it self-sufficiency in food, clothing and shelter...The goal seemed to become more elusive in recent years as the price of Guyana's basic commodities - sugar, rice and bauxite - fell sharply in international markets.
>
> Mr. Burnham's Government had been losing popularity in recent years as the financial crisis made it difficult to import even such basic foods as wheat flour. (Meislin, 1985 p.9)[4]

It was a truly tough time for the people and everyone scraped by with as much as they could. It was also during these moments, that we saw friendships built and love truly expressed.

---

[4] Meislin, Richard J. "Guyana's Leader Dies; Successor Is Sworn In.", *The New York Times,* New York. August 7, 1985. Accessed: September 16, 2019.

Whether it was sharing in a fisherman's catch, an extra egg here, an extra vegetable there, or the baking of an extra loaf of bread for a neighbor's evening meal, it was done out of the goodness of one's heart. It was those acts of thoughtfulness and kindness that I'll never forget for it made me see the love and resilience in humanity that some displayed even in the darkest of times.

15 GEORGETOWN

"Children, Children!" Daddy called out to us. "We're going on a special trip into town today. Uncle will give us a ride. Suh get ready fast," he said.

"Ok, Daddy! we said excitedly. "Abi guh hurry."

"It's a really special day!" he said with a wide grin.

Soon, the seven of us were packed into a car with our Uncle. My brother was squeezed in the middle seat between my Uncle and Dad and the rest of us were in the back with our mother.

"Remember, sit one in and one out," said my father, carefully instructing us on the most functional way to travel that day.

"One in, One out!" That was the famous phrase that he used years later in the US when he purchased his first car and we all filed into the back seat. It is also the phrase that we would look back at and smile as we remember the precious moments he gave to us and the good times we shared together as a family.

Plunk Plunk Plunk went the tires of the small truck before us as it rattled and rolled over the Demerara Harbour Bridge. Built on pontoons, the bridge make a loud cackling noise when vehicles drove on top. It is one of the world's longest floating bridges and connects the people of West Bank Demerara to Guyana's capital, Georgetown.

My heart sank as our car creaked down the main entrance of the ramp. The bridge was so low that I felt as if we would sink or float away along with the barrels that I saw drifting around the water. Traffic was light but steady. We stopped for a moment as part of the drawbridge lifted to allow water ferries passing by.

I was nervous the whole ride and silently prayed that we would make it across safely. It was only when our vehicle touched the paved road that I was finally able to relax.

The city was noisy but exciting. People hustled to and fro across the busy streets. Most of them on their way to work. I saw a few men and women impeccably dressed in their tailored suits and long flowing dresses with colorful purses or dark briefcases clutched tightly by their side.

Two sets of parents walked by holding hands with their little tots while a young couple strolled along the street together, looking happy and in-love. A youth rode his bicycle along the sidewalk while construction workers in hard hats were on the opposite side of us, drilling and moving large boulders from the road.

I peeked out the car's window just as we were passing the beautiful St. Andrew's Cathedral, one of tallest wooden structures left on earth. I marveled at its architecture and envisioned myself one day inside of its corridors.

As we sped along, the Umana Yana, [5]an Amerindian heritage site came into view. It is a thatched

---

[5] Hernandez, Lennox J. "The Story of Umana Yana: A Preliminary Chronicle of Guyana's Umana Yanas. " *Guyana Times International.* (Georgetown, Guyana) September 25, 2015. Acessed: September 19, 2019

roof monument with a wide circular base that was built

entirely of dried leaves and straw without the use of nails.

This skillful construct was designed by the indigenous

Wai Wai's, one of the nine Amerindian tribes that grace

Guyana's shores and is a testament of the many skills and

contributions that they have made to the Guyanese

society.

We waved goodbye to our uncle who kindly

dropped us off and went off to work then headed into the

US Embassy, that was next door to the Umana Yana.

"Now everyone behave yuhself." Mom quietly

ordered as we fidgeted by her side. "Everyone, pay

attention and do exactly what the mister tells you."

We stood in line, careful not to make a sound as the armed guard called out to us one by one. It was my turn next and he led me to a chair behind a large white screen.

"Sit just right there," he said, then walked back to where my parents were.

A sweet lady with a camera came by. She stood at a distance and took my picture from the front and sides.

"You are all set, sweetie. Now run to mommy … and good luck in America," she said with a smile.

The process at the Embassy was tedious and long as people seemed to be packed to capacity as they waited on line for their own visas, passport or pictures. Most of us were tired and hungry from the long trip. Afterwards, our family decided to grab a quick bite to eat at a fancy Chinese restaurant and happily partook in the aromatic delicacies they had to offer such as Steamed Dumplings, Chow Mein, Fried Chicken and Fried Rice. We hurried back home on the evening bus so that we could reach before the night fell.

On the way there, I spotted the central hub of Guyana's commerce, the thriving Stabroek Market with its large crowds and beaming tower that reached high into the sky with a clock in its center. It was packed with merchants selling a variety of fresh seafood, meat, vegetables and fruits. It was also the New York's fifth avenue of Guyana where people went to gain the most desirable products. In the market, people traded cloths, spices, goods and artifacts both locally and from our neighboring countries.

Our car turned into Revolution Square. There, a large statue of Cuffy[6] appeared. Cuffy was a brave man, cruelly captured from West Africa and brought to work as a slave in Berbice by Dutch colonists. In 1763, he led a successful revolt that included over 2500 slaves and eventually became a governor of Guyana. His story is etched in stone forever and stands proudly as a heroic reminder of one man's quest for freedom against all odds.

The next trip into town would be our last and most treasurable. This time we took the ferry and my heart was completely at ease throughout the trip. Our trip

---

[6] Ramsay, Rehanna. "Cuffy-A Symbol of Struggle and Freedom." *Kaieteur News,* July 28th, 2013 Accessed: September 19, 2019 https://www.kaieteurnewsonline.com/2013/07/28/cuffy-a-symbol-of-struggle-and-freedom/

was to Guyana's beautiful Botanical Gardens and Zoo that held an array of exotic plants, flowers and exciting wildlife in its pristine Amazonian jungle.

The garden was a tropical paradise that created an ambiance of peace and serenity throughout its path. I'll never forget walking over the famous Kissing Bridge where dreamy lovers and newlyweds held hands and embraced then kissed to symbolize their special unity. It was a sweet gesture of love that as a child, I had only read about in fairytales. Aside from the breathtaking Kaieteur Falls, the Kissing Bridge is one of Guyana's top romantic backdrops.

Further up the paved pathway sits a lily pond with the glorious Victoria regalia lilies, Guyana's national flower, blooming happily on top. I stood there for a moment and stared at the beautiful flower not knowing that sometime in the future, that flower would hold a special significance when I chose a name for my precious baby girl.

As we entered the zoological park, I could already hear the singing birds in the trees and smell the fresh scent of rain as the skies began to darken. We had to move fast. A few drops drizzled on top of my head as I stayed close to my other siblings.

Soon we caught sight of a large owl with wide eyes that stared right into our soul. It fluffed its feathers and turned its head as if to tell us to be on our way. More birds of the rainforest fluttered into sight including a noisy toucan and an orange parrot.

A manatee peeked its head from a pond and we caught sight of the magnificent jaguar and tapir. I stayed far away from the reptiles such as the crocodile and the anacondas which I knew would haunt my dreams for days to come.

Big drops of rain began bursting from the cloud and we poured out the park to seek shelter. The bus pulled up just in time and we took it over the bridge once more. I fell asleep a few minutes after we found a seat and as such my ride home was pleasant and sweet.

16 TIMEHRI AIRPORT

The night before we left Guyana, there were lots of people who crammed into our little house. They sat on the floor and talked of a bright future ahead in America, especially for the children. Suitcases were opened and filled with just a few pieces of clothing. The people brought sponge and fruit cakes and parting gifts, small tokens of affection that symbolized their friendship with my family which were included with our bags as well. Sometime during the night, the kids fell asleep and the adults stayed up.

Just before dawn, the house was serene and silent for everyone had left. My siblings and I dressed in the outfits my mom had prepared for us. I wore a white collared shirt, a pink silk skirt and a matching jacket. My brothers wore their little gray suits with vests. When we were finished, we looked like little darlings ready for a formal portrait.

When we reached Timehri (now Cheddi Jagan) International Airport, our Aunt, Uncle and four cousins were anxiously waiting for us in the baggage check-in area. They were happy and excited for our trip and to experience a country that we had only dreamed of.

My grandmother hugged me very tightly and gave me a kiss on the cheek before I skipped off to join the rest of my family. As I looked back, I saw the trickle of tears down her cheeks. I would never see my grandmother again but I have never forgotten that day nor the love she showed to me as a child. That would stay with me forever and so would the place I once called home...*GUYANA*.

EPILOGUE

I was 10 years old when my family emigrated to the United States. I'll never forget the excitement I felt when I looked out the window of Guyana Airways and saw the gleaming lights of the New York City skyline. I was completely mesmerized by the sight and even more anxious to discover what awaited my family and I in this beautiful city. The plane made a sharp turn and I could hear the roar of the engine and feel the sudden drop as it descended in the direction of JFK's runway.

September 10th, 2014

My Birthday

Brooklyn Heights Promenade

It is a cool and breezy summer afternoon as I sit on a lone bench on the Promenade. The sun is high in the sky. Its rays beam down on the glistening waters below. The New York Harbor is busy today as traffic navigates the waters. I watch as the little boats float by followed by water taxis, a cargo ship and a cruise line. Somewhere in the corner of the bank are a group of people on jet skis ready to propel themselves forward in a riveting race. A

helicopter hovers in the near distance. I stare out at the
tall buildings dotting the New York Skyline.

A man holding a cute little Maltese walks by just
as a lady in blue jeans and a yellow tank top blocks my
view. She has a camera around her neck and saunters by
snapping as she goes. I get up to leave but decide to take
in the sight a little closer to the river. With my hand on
the rails, my eyes move to my far left where Lady
Liberty stands with a crown on her head and her torch
held high. I reflect on what she truly stands for, a beacon
of hope and freedom for all who reach her shore. At her
feet is the famous poem by Emma Lazarus, "Give me
your tired, your poor, your huddled masses yearning to
breathe free, The wretched refuse of your teeming shore.
Send these, the homeless, tempest-tossed to me, I lift my
lamp beside the golden door! "These words mean so

much to me. I am deeply humbled as I think of the many people who have arrived on this land seeking a better life for themselves and their children. I think of my own family who was one of them.

With five children, all under the age of 10, my parents arrived safely in the United States on a cold and wintry day, escaping the racial turmoil and political unrest that lay at the height of Guyana's new election. For all of us, a new life, a new chapter had begun. Looking up at the Statue of Liberty, I am reminded of how far I've come, of what I have yet to achieve, and of what remains in my heart of the land I once left behind.

ABOUT THE AUTHOR

Abigail Satnarine an active member of the Indo-Guyanese community and an advocate for Women's and Children's Rights. She holds a BA from St. John's University in English and her Master of Science degree in Global Affairs at New York University with a concentration in Human Rights and International Law. She is the author of, "The Story of Two Boys: A Tale of Two Lives and How One Life Greatly Impacted the Other," a deeply personal book and inspiring short story dedicated to her late father. She is also a lover of the arts and culture and mom to a beautiful little girl who is her light and love every day. She resides in New York with her husband and child.

CPSIA information can be obtained
at www.ICGtesting.com
Printed in the USA
LVHW061153141019
634126LV00030B/6825/P